FUNDAMENTAL THINGS APPLY
Reflecting on Christian Basics
CLYDE F. CREWS

AVE MARIA PRESS
NOTRE DAME, INDIANA 46556

Permissions and Credits:

Excerpts from "Choruses from 'The Rock' " in COLLECTED POEMS 1909-1962 by T. S. Eliot are reprinted by permission of Harcourt Brace Jovanovich, Inc.; copyright 1936 by Harcourt Brace Jovanovich, Inc.; copyright © 1963, 1964 by T. S. Eliot.

Excerpts from "For the Time Being, A Christmas Oratorio" in W. H. AUDEN: COLLECTED POEMS edited by Edward Mendelson are reprinted by permission of Random House, Inc.; copyright © 1976.

Unless otherwise indicated, all scripture quotes are excerpted from THE JERUSALEM BIBLE, copyright © 1966 by Darton, Longman & Todd, Ltd. and Doubleday & Company, Inc. Used with permission of the publisher.

International Standard Book Number: 0-87793-274-3 (Cloth)
0-87793-272-7 (Paper)

Library of Congress Catalog Card Number: 83-71005

Printed and bound in the United States of America.

Cover and text design: Carol A. Robak

◆ contents

Contents

4

◉foreword

As we approach the turn of the century, the call to celebrate such human achievements as our adventures in space and the development of sophisticated computers and communications systems also invites us to intensify our desire to enter deeply into another pursuit—a pursuit, which through our own creativity, will allow us to become more fully human.

A recent magazine ad summarizes well this new pursuit. The words simply read, THE NEW FRONTIER OF THE SPACE AGE: INNER SPACE.

We live in a time threatened with the loss of a sense of inwardness. Amidst the noise, the ceaseless activity and the complexity of a technological society, we may forget that all that is outside of us has no meaning of its own. Meaning flows from the inside out.

Meaning does not come all at once; it grows in nearly imperceptible ways. For something to have meaning for us, it must be taken into ourselves and, through a process of self-reflection, be submitted to an inner scrutiny that is possible only in times of quiet and external inactivity.

Foreword

The times in which we live do not, of themselves, call us to journey in inner space. We need people who will invite us to notice the life that is around us with a message so powerful that it will leap from noticing the life around us to tending the life within us. Jesus often said to his followers, "Do you know that the kingdom is within you?"

The call to the regions of inner space is not an invitation to the narcissism which is apparent in certain segments of society. We make the inner journey in pursuit of meaning only so that we may live in this world as channels of hope and healing. Only through the costly adventure into inner space can we hope to bring the wisdom that is necessary to discover the implications for us as Christians of the ventures into outer space.

Self-reflection and turning to God in prayer are fundamental to full human life. Without self-reflection human actions become at best simply repetitious and, at worst, even destructive. To see where we are going, to determine where we wish to go, we must be attentive to where we have been.

Of all the "fundamental things that apply" perhaps the greatest of these is our ability to respond to a series of meditations such as these by Father Clyde Crews. He offers a way to be more fully aware and more consciously responsive to our God and to life. As turning to the sun is fundamental to the life of a green plant, as turning to the presence of a friend is vital to life for each of us, so turning to the God within us prepares us and enables us to share the life that is ours.

PAULA RIPPLE, F.S.P.A.

◆introduction

◆ legacies

In 1942, the second world war was convulsing and devastating the people of the earth; the Holocaust went relentlessly on its blasphemous and genocidal way; research advanced rapidly among the Americans and Germans on the nuclear weaponry that often would make the postwar world a waking nightmare.

In that same epochal year, in fact on Thanksgiving Day, Warner Studios in the United States released a film that was to become a cinematic classic and winner of the 1943 Oscar—*Casablanca*. At the emotional epicenter of this war film, Dooley Wilson sings "As Time Goes By," a ballad written by Herman Hupfeld in 1931. "The fundamental things apply," the lyric insists, "as time goes by."

A nice sentiment, surely. But are there, in fact, stabilities and fidelities to be held to in such a world as we now inhabit? As early as 1929, Walter Lippmann wrote a sort of new testament of insecurity in *A Preface to Morals* with such dispiriting titles as "Whirl Is King," and "The Dissolution of the Ancestral Order." Ten years later, W. H. Auden surveyed the scene of the 1930's, supposedly chastened by economic disaster, and pronounced it all in "September 1, 1939" to have been "a low dishonest decade."

From the literature of the existentialist—Camus reinvoking poor old Sisyphus in his repetitive though pointless life task—down to the recent *Fate of the Earth* by Jonathan Schell, we have been made aware over and over that we are, as Barbara Tuchman wrote of the 1300's, a "century born to woe." Historical parallels may fascinate us and cushion our fears and anxieties, but we cannot kid ourselves for long. People have suffered terribly before in history, and no doubt may suffer terribly again. But for sheer pace of personal, professional and societal change; for future shock, turmoil, terror and ultimate danger, the 20th century is without parallel.

The brush may be too thick with the dark tones. In these same years there have also been accomplishments, opportunities and points of hope. Probably no more hopeful corporate international voice is to be found in the 20th century than that of the Second Vatican Council with its perceptive opening sections of *The Church in the Modern World* (1965).

Amid all the verbal clutter of this often unhappy century, it may well be the religious voices that have been most consistently balanced on the jagged edge of realism—fending off both presumption and despair. It was Thomas Merton who spoke of the primal religious and moral necessity of being human in this most inhuman of times. His voice has been one of a chorus that has included the likes of Abraham Heschel, Martin Luther King, Jr., Dag Hammarskjold, Dorothy Day, Paul Tillich, Dietrich Bonhoeffer, Flannery O'Connor and Karl Rahner.

It has long been the task of religion to make us aware of our infirmities before we can seek a saving remedy. T. S. Eliot wrote in *Choruses from "The Rock"* (1934):

Introduction

Why should men love the Church? Why
   should they
      love her laws?
She tells them of Life and Death, and of all
   that
      they would forget.
She is tender where they would be hard, and
   hard
      where they like to be soft.
She tells them of Evil and Sin and other
   unpleasant
      facts.

That same church, Eliot continues, also reminds
humanity of the possibility to which grace has
called it: a life more abundant.

As far as Christianity—or any great
religion—is concerned, fundamental things do apply. The Psalms constitute a troubled symphony of
trust in God despite the most dire of contrary appearances. And the tempestuous Paul often points
out in his most cosmic imagery that no external
horrors—even the pounding force of death
itself—can split apart the power for goodness at the
heart of God and reality. In Gerard Manley
Hopkins' simple and unforgettable line in "God's
Grandeur"—"There lives the dearest freshness deep
down things."

A contemporary of Hopkins', though much
better known by his age, was Matthew Arnold. As
early as 1853 the perceptive poet and social critic
had written in "The Scholar Gipsy":

Thou waitest for the spark from heaven:
   and we,
Vague half-believers of our casual creeds,

10

Who never deeply felt, nor clearly willed,
Whose insight never has borne fruit in deeds,
Whose weak resolves never have been
    fulfilled;
For whom each year we see
Breeds new beginnings, disappointments new;
Who hesitate and falter life away,
And lose tomorrow the ground won today—
Ah, do not we, wanderer, await it too?

What follows in these unsystematic pages is an attempt to explore themes of some of the fundamental things—deep down things. If there is a motif that runs throughout these essays, it is the conviction that our religious traditions—Catholic Christianity in particular—have shaping words to say to us as individuals and as a people. We remain half-believers and possessors of casual creeds to our own personal, religious and social peril. While we, too, await the spark from heaven, we also remain—for all our faltering—a people wobbly, but erect: a set of dry bones, perhaps, but still capable of the fire of the Spirit and the burst of life.

Our creeds of old are, in truth, creeds of the new—if we know how to listen to the holy writings, traditions, experiences and relationships, the saints and sinners, the voice of God that may speak in our turmoil as well as in our peace. These creeds and the traditions they represent point to rich legacies—revelations and insights that help us to find a kind of dynamic stability in an unquiet, sometimes chaotic time.

In exploring fidelity, hope, suffering and several other themes, we attend to the fundamental things that apply whatever the economic or political or metaphysical season. In seeking out such aspects of life, one may be privileged to look within, around and beyond the self to the very heart of reality.

To enter into our own mystery is to enter as well into the mystery of that Lord who is both our ground and our goal. And to enter into that inexhaustible mystery is to come to life in its complexity—body and soul—and to revel totally in God our Savior.

CLYDE F. CREWS
Louisville
Feast of the Assumption

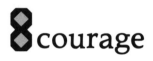courage

◆ grace under pressure

Our English word "courage" has its roots in the Middle-English *corage*, the French *coeur*, and the Latin *cor*. All mean "heart" and all carry the connotation of stoutheartedness. They suggest firmness of resolve, identity and commitment in the face of opposition.

Courage has long been listed as one of the four classical cardinal virtues—alongside prudence, justice, and temperance. These were recognized qualities of character in the Greco-Roman world, and Christianity was pleased to elaborate them as part of its own values network.

Paul Tillich, the great Lutheran theologian, saw in the virtue of courage the central thread of the human fabric and discussed it at length in his pivotal work of 1952, *The Courage To Be.* John F. Kennedy in *Profiles in Courage* declared it to be "the most admirable of human virtues." And Ernest Hemingway, in a treasured phrase, called it "grace under pressure."

In one of its more exigetically mysterious little scenes, the New Testament images the fortitude of Jesus in the scene of the woman taken in adultery. Only John presents the story, and most commentators judge it out of place in the Johannine narrative, more like a Synoptic story that wandered across an evangelical county line. Yet, a strong case can be made for its historical worth.

The Pharisees, a conservative lay group, tended to equate depth of religious commitment with rigid observance of the law. It was this rigidity that would trouble Paul when he made his famous distinction between the letter and spirit of the law.

This group of Pharisees now tries an intimidation tactic on Jesus. They seem intent on trapping him in a tough political and theological situation. If he doesn't agree with their harsh reading of the affair, they will be able to charge loudly and long that he isn't a good Jew. If, on the other hand, he ends up being a party to the execution they are so eager to initiate, his support among the crowds will erode rapidly.

And so the stage is set for one of the most pointed short stories presented in the New Testament. Jesus exemplifies in this one short piece all four of the great virtues: prudence, justice, temperance and above all, fortitude or courage. He refuses to allow either the Pharisees or the crowd to set his agenda. He refuses to allow the unfortunate woman to be turned into a political pawn. In fact he is the only one to speak to the woman calmly and critically, yet kindly. There is a grand nonverbal drama in which Jesus then writes on the sand or ground, the only reference to Jesus writing in the entire New Testament.

What a scene is this. With an angry crowd and a terrified woman before him, Jesus leans down to trace on the ground. The turmoil around him continues. He straightens up long enough to deliver his epochal lines that those without sin should cast the first stone. This was a brilliant, prudent touch. He leans down again. The crowd begins to slip away "beginning with the oldest," presumably because Jesus might be writing their secret faults, and the eldest might have more to repent.

The second time Jesus stands upright, only the woman remains. He temperately renders her a healing word, but also makes the stiff demand of refraining from sin in the future.

This, then, represented Jesus of Nazareth's style of courage. His commitment to the troubled person did not depend on the mood of the crowd or the tenor of times. His kindness was not limited by his own mood or disposition. His drive for justice was not deflected by whichever way the political or economic winds seemed to be blowing. He stood for that which ought to be, in season and out.

Here is one of many examples from the New Testament of grace under pressure. Christian history and the stories of countless other religious and humane people provide their own ennobling accounts—sometimes bracing, sometimes chilling—of humanity at its best. That mettle lies deep in all people, a gift and grace of God. Even the weary frustrations and upsets of everyday life cannot completely obscure this deep-set inner possibility. In our own faulting ways, we could convert our latent life-courage into a potent force for the good.

It was another American writer, Mark Twain, who commented that true courage lay not in the absence of fear, but in significant action in the face of it. That is the genuine meaning of heartiness. And in its truest sense, such courage represents grace under pressure.

death

◈ trustful dying

In Robert Bolt's *A Man For All Seasons*, Sir Thomas More appears in the last scene standing on the scaffold awaiting execution. He draws his daughter Margaret in his arms and speaks these words:

> Have patience, Margaret, and trouble not yourself. Death comes for us all. Even at our birth—even at our birth, death does but stand aside a little. And every day he looks toward us and muses somewhat to himself whether that day or the next he will draw nigh. It is the law of nature and the will of God.

Death invariably comes with a sting and a shock—whether it be suddenly swift or long dreaded and expected. It has been called the grim reaper and the great leveller. Death is also the term of our days that makes all things precious. For the trusting Christian, it is the total investment of self we ultimately make in order to enter that range of greater coherence and intensity for which we strive all of our mortal days.

It matters not unduly whether at the moment of death we are young or old, rich or poor, if it is summer or winter. It matters only that life has been good, and that we are willing to have given ourselves completely to the venture of life until God's moment is upon us. At that moment we let go of the lesser reality of our smaller selves to be enfolded and swaddled into the wider reality we are yet to be, caressed by that very love that wears so many disguises.

For this we were born. For this we came into the world: to perceive at the crucial points of our lives that the tenderness of which Christianity speaks is the very truth about life itself and not ultimately illusion. It becomes the great privilege of a life to learn that it is not the fool who believes and hopes, but the realist, the questioner, and the lover.

In short, death can be perceived as a kind of birth. Like all beginnings and like all things worthwhile, it exacts a cost of process and pain. Jesus insisted that those who would gain their lives must lose them. He proclaimed that unless the seed fall in the earth and die, the grain will never grow. His whole life was an affirmation that death does not have the final say on the face of the earth. Paul echoed the theme: Death, where is your victory? Where is your sting?

Yet, unavoidably, death seems to be the time of the troubling of hearts. It causes us to begin to see things in a shattering perspective. Things will not always be what they are. We are destined to pass beyond what we know. And the unknown always brings its weight of anxiety and fears.

And yet, all of us without exception are called to be about the business of trustful dying. "Do not let your hearts be troubled." Jesus has walked the way, and felt the darkness before us. He is like the kindly parent or the trusted friend who has gone a way ahead in a strange situation or a new town to prepare things for us so that we will feel at home. "I am going to prepare a place for you."

Jesus has become the way:
—by standing faithfully to his task,
—by loving the earth and its people and its
   possibilities,
—by trusting the utter kindness of God.
Jesus' way leads *through* this life, but also more deeply *into* this life and at last *beyond* this life, into a fuller dimension of reality.

The Jewish Talmud offers a marvelous meditation on trustful dying. Why is it, the holy book asks, that all of us come into the world with clenched fists, but usually leave it with opened fingers? Perhaps because at last we have learned that life itself is a gift from God. Wise people live life to the full while it is theirs. They grow in it, develop, and bring their own absolutely unique coloring to the kaleidoscope of the earth. But they dare not clutch at it, smother it, or desperately keep a grip.

In letting go, in letting the hand speak to God of readiness and trust, we utter our last, and perhaps our truest prayer. And the God who hears every faithful call will surely attend to this one. It is Bolt's St. Thomas More who once again speaks the hopeful and sobering words: "I go to God; He would not refuse one so blithe to see Him."

◆a darkness of threats and promises

> None of us lives as his own master and none of
> us dies as his own master.
>
> Romans 14:7 (NAB)

Few words have ever been spoken—religious or
otherwise—that can sear so deeply with their simple truthfulness.

We are never fully in control of our own
lives—this is both part of our majesty and part of
our misery. We are born and continue to live only
because we are in a lifetime web of giving and
receiving. Each unrepeatable day of our lives is a
gift that we have not quite earned. St. Ignatius said
so pointedly in the 16th century those words that
still shore us up today: it matters not whether we
live a long life or a short life, only if it be a good
and intense life.

Still, anyone who has sensitivities at all has
come to grips with death in a somewhat less
philosophic fashion. That is to say, it is part of
maturity itself to be aware of life's cutting edge. To
know the frustrations and sufferings of living is, on
many days, to know much about dying. We see the
good die young. We see those who struggle for a
better life vexed and opposed. We see the very best
twisted and crucified. This is the darkness "heavy
in promises and threats," as Teilhard de Chardin
once described it, which Christians are called to il-
luminate with glimmers of the divine presence.

What a bleak picture it would all be if Christianity didn't live under the sign of the cross: the
sign of contradiction. This means an assurance that

all of us will somehow suffer, but it means also the even greater assurance that suffering doesn't end in its own misery. It can become a passage that leads to inner depth, compassion, sensitivity, perspective and peace. In short, suffering can point the way to resurrection.

Is not faith, in its most elementary proclamation, the assurance that things are more than they seem to be? If life were lived only on its surface, hope would be at a discount and even grief itself would be pointless. But our most profound human experiences cry out that promise is ultimately more important to humanity than profit; that such intangibles as hope, endurance, and compassion count more mightily on the earth than evil and even death.

It was in his *Christmas Oratorio* during the catastrophic war year of 1944 that W. H. Auden wrote:

> We who must die demand a miracle
> How could the eternal do a temporal act,
> The infinite become a finite fact?
> Nothing can save us that is possible.
> We who must die demand a miracle.

Death and life fold into one another. The ordinary and the miraculous, too, are blended in our human experience. But humanity through all its history has cried out for the ultimate miracle that our lives have meaning and that they might be stronger than death. It is precisely our experience of the depths and unexpected possibilities of ordinary life that disposes us to believe that a life beyond the limits of this one seems neither farfetched nor desperate.

Nothing can save us that is possible. As human beings, we are not the source of our own sufficiency. We are not our own masters. In life and death, Christianity insists, we belong to the Lord. To belong to Jesus is to enter his life, his suffering, his perspectives, his trust, and ultimately his dying.

In drawing humanity beyond the appearance of death to the utter sufficiency of life, the Christ teaches us that life belongs ultimately to life, and not to death. We who are not our own masters demand a miracle. And the miracle is already there, deep within, ready to emerge and erupt. The one who is our master and our steady hope has made that his primary task and promise.

fidelity

◆ we are not our own

C. S. Lewis, who described himself in 1929 as "the most reluctant convert in all of England," was finally drawn into religious faith when a brief line of George Macdonald's haunted him: "the one principle of hell is—I am my own."

In some ways, Macdonald had simply restated one of the primal sins: the insistence that we may select the frame and total destiny of the self; that we can seize life and twist it about until it resembles that which the narrow self wishes it to be.

Such a position denies that the self is ultimately linked both in life and death to a wider realm of significance. Rather, it would hold that we belong totally to ourselves alone, our primary allegiance satisfied when the individual is physically or emotionally sated.

But life is vaster, more frightening, and more enticing than that. To be is to be linked. In the beginning, as the great Jewish writer Martin Buber reminded us, is relationship.

We are further reminded by another great writer of our century, Gabriel Marcel, a French convert to Catholicism, that we are the only creatures on the earth who make promises. Such promising, in fact, is one of the fundamental ways that we enter into relationships with others. Such human pledges take root and make sense only because God in turn is the ultimate promiser, grounding all that we do, say, hope or imagine.

To live out a life that is profoundly human, then, is to have to make choices:

of relatedness	over	isolation,
of promise	over	scepticism,
of fidelity	over	futility.

The time of marriage for religious people is a time of special intensity precisely because it is a time of promises, human and divine. Such a solemn yet joyous moment is also an invitation to reaffirm those truths and values of faith that give life the salt and savor it so badly needs if it is to be truly worth living.

Especially in America today, a seriously intended marriage is a marvel and a privilege. In the midst of our weaknesses and vulnerabilities, there are still those who can gather the courage and strength to cast their future in some manner into the life of another, and into the life of a Lord who bids them to become promisers and lovers in the first place.

In the middle of a nation that at times seems to have forgotten the meaning of the word trust, we still find men and women eager to pledge a lasting trust to one another and to their community. In the whirlwind of future shock and change that is late 20th-century America, believers are still ready to speak with their lives of ageless values of permanence and persistence.

They make of their lives a *covenant*, a reality rich in Jewish and early Christian scriptural associations. In *hesed* relationships, one joins another with unending familial identity and commitments. One finite human life is joined irrevocably to another, and finds the grace and courage to say forever. So solemn a promise is possible precisely because the two are more than themselves, either as individuals or as couple. They are, in covenant, touching and touched by the infinite intimacy, constancy and mystery of God's very life.

By joining their lives together, such couples, while remaining the wonder of their own unique selves, also become a new reality together—a force in our midst for the doing of good. By their promises and proclaimings, they seek to put behind them greediness and apathy, coldness and indifference. They pledge to become a new warm center of creativity, sharing and compassion in the troubled human community of our anxious age.

And if they signal hope to us, such lovers also speak to us of realism. If they are wise, they surely know that married life folds within itself ecstasies and frustrations, expectancies and disappointments. Yet, they are aware that such insecurities are the price one pays in a venture with so high a possible yield.

Ultimately, a mature couple truly in faith and in love allows God to be more fully present to one another and to us all. That is, after all, a core meaning of sacrament: God getting in touch with men and women through the presences, risks, signs, works and fibers of the human.

Trust, permanence, compassion, endurance, joy—these are timeless things we say and celebrate in every Christian marriage. To stand around a couple at such a time is to stand on the sacred ground of human choice and more-than-human possibility. Truly, it is a time to pledge and to pray, to reflect and to revel.

◆chosen passions

In the fascination, even obsession, of our society with all things sexual—from creative ways of human coupling to every conceivable form of erotic expression—proponents of Christian marriage have found it necessary to sharpen both their wits and their articulations. And if our society is finding marriage a tad traditional, even passé, it looks upon the chaste single life, especially based on religious or clerical commitment, as beyond any comprehensible pale.

And yet, the ability of countless men and women to opt for a life of carefully chosen and directed intensities without genital issue has been, and continues to be, an integrated, fulfilling, even passionate way of living a mature life. To call to mind only those celibates who have abused their humanity so badly as to become indifferent, cold, grasping, domineering or selfish, is to forget the historical army of well-adjusted religious or lay singles. It is also to fail to note the amazing array of sexual athletes over the eons who have fallen easy prey to the very same moral and emotional maladies that are said to afflict "bachelors and old maids."

Especially, a word needs to be said in tribute to those believers who—revering the incarnational and sacramental energies of sexuality in others—have chosen singleness or life in community for themselves. Their choice may be woven of many motivational strands, yet displays a predominant pattern that enriches both their own lives and that of the human family. Their archetype for such enrichment is the Christ who came to bring life to the full to all people of all stations and conditions. In short, there exists even within a society such as our own, a kind of marriage parallel, a chosen or vowed life that, like marriage, calls forth love, commitment, service, creativity, sacrifice and spirituality.

Who are some of these people who have gone before us, and still mingle among us, though in numbers smaller than in some earlier generations? Far from being lifeless ciphers, they live out their own special fidelity to life by often being salty, resolute, rollicking people whose faith and hope and compassion have sunk into their very beings and have become infectious for others. They have been men and women who know how to suffer and how to serve; how to weep with force and laugh with a mighty roar. They have proved themselves fit runners in the human race and stand in need of no elaborate modern apologetic. They have been patient, steady, self-possessed, faithful and true.

The single religious shares in the burden, responsibility, excitement and frustration of the vast human enterprise—standing in our midst *not* to be signs as such, but to be committed and loyal with a vital Christic vision of life's qualities and possibilities.

The fundamental life task of the single religious is always the transformation of the self under the lead of the befriending Spirit. From such a primal re-spiriting of the self there flows a life dedicated to service. From this lifestyle, a distinctive sign value may well arise. But just as in the faithful marriage, one chooses and works first at the reality; the sign flows on its own and is not chosen for itself.

What sign or signal might the community read from the celibate life? It could be risky to say: signs get mixed and signals get crossed. Yet, it is possible to see a flesh-and-blood awareness that even beyond the powerful goods of personal satisfaction and family strengths, there are human and spiritual realities worth pondering, and searching and reaching for.

The Catholic sensibility in particular seems to need some people present who have based their lives radically—at root—on the promise that this world is pregnant with a reality greater than itself. Marriage says this in its own way, of course. Still, the witness of Christian centuries is that the balanced life of Christian singleness has its own specially powerful manner, its own quietly articulate way, of bringing life to life.

Ranks of book shelves have been laden with attempts to define this reality of celibacy, usually with minimal efficacy. It is as notoriously hard to define as the love of which it is so specially and intimately a manifestation. It may well be that we have never advanced beyond Augustine's insistence in the *City of God* in the fifth century that the main drive of a life is in finding what is worthy of love and how we go about loving that reality. Life, married or single, is a matter of passion, a gift of a God whose inner reality is interpersonal and whose creative energy *is*, without the possibility of exhaustion.

Fundamental Things Apply

Life is—or ought to be—
Passions well-wrought:
Given and received,
Hunted and bestowed.
Chosen passions,
Now diffuse, now intense,
Steady and relentless.
Excluding others as
Identity's price.

Not to know all
Is to know much.
And more.

holiness

◆ the ancient faith and the modern age

To an age alive with possibilities and progress, yet
more than ever aware of its fragility and brokenness . . .

> *Christianity humbly points to the compas-*
> *sionate Lord and his presence to humanity*
> *in word and sacrament, creed and prayer,*
> *fidelity and forgiveness, leadership and*
> *community.*

To a world that offers people the dismal
prospect that things are only what they seem to
be . . .

> *The Christian faith cries out for human*
> *totality, and for hidden wholeness. It*
> *speaks not only of the dignity of each per-*
> *son and of every person, but it urges that*
> *precisely in their love and creativity men*
> *and women come closest to their God.*

To a society concerned with affluence and
clutching, with an attachment to appearances,
busyness and power for its own sake . . .

> *The Christian churches speak of sparing-*
> *ness, simplicity and the commitment to*
> *sharing; thus they hope to evoke a silence in*
> *which the word of God may fruitfully*
> *speak.*

To a generation that has lost hold of heroes
and heroines who might electrify their lives and
lead them forth from their lesser selves . . .

> *The Christian tradition enshrines the living*
> *witness of the saints, those countless men*

*and women through the centuries who have
come to God in a myriad of ways through
their often stumbling lives.*

To a theological era alive with ecumenical
hope and honest religious search . . .

*Christianity invites all believers and honest
men and women to join together in concern
for "the joys and hopes, the griefs and
anxieties of this age," and to "champion the
Godlike seed which has been sown" in all
humanity. (The Church in the Modern
World.)*

To restless men and women of the unquiet
city surrounded by insecurity and confusion . . .

*The Christian heritage proclaims rootedness
in a long heritage of unity and diversity,
authority and freedom, creativity and tradition.*

To all those who would use their faith as
some sanctuary from the social force of the gospel
and its demands . . .

*Christianity sounds a constant call for peace
flowing from the work of justice and social
involvement.*

To those fearful people who fail to revel
with their whole being in God their Savior as did
the mother of the Lord Jesus . . .

*Christian humanism declares that "nothing
genuinely human fails to raise an echo" in
the Christian heart (The Church in the
Modern World). It also proclaims the call of
the Lord through all the energies of men and*

women at their finest: education and the arts, science and sport, labor and humor, honest differences and genuine peace.

And to those men and women today who lead lives of gentle strength and quiet greatness; to those who are poor in spirit and burn with care over the hungry, the sick, the lonely and the misunderstood; to those good parents who devote their best energies to their children; to those who suffer persecution for justice' sake and make their lives mercy in a hardened time . . .

Christianity beckons as a quiet haven and pilgrim's rest. Here the befriending Spirit points the way for the weary to the fullness of the Father's consolation.

◆ totality

What Mary, mother of the Lord, has become—and Catholic Christianity celebrates this in the feast of the Assumption—the Christian people are seeking yet to be. She provides a realistic hope of what can result when the fullness of grace is joined with simple and penetrating human goodness.

Mary was, by all accounts recorded of her, a faithful, seasoned and well-tempered woman. Everything that we know of her from scripture (and she is mentioned only occasionally) portrays a rare and striking woman. She has been disserved in Christian history by neglect in some quarters and by an excessive and oversentimentalized regard in others. She was, in truth, remarkable as a woman in her own right; as the mother who doubtlessly instilled in the young Jesus a love for the profundity of Judaism; and as the steady and stouthearted believer in Jesus, even in the darkest of times.

What do we know of this holy woman whom the scriptures call "highly favored" of the Lord?

She was a woman of critical faith. As the account in Luke clearly shows, she was the servant and truster of the Lord. Yet, she was quite competent at interrogating the messenger of that same Lord. She was also not above prodding and challenging her son in his own ministry. Her faith was strong and mature, but hardly unquestioning.

She was a woman of great compassion for the needs and feelings of others. This is evidenced not only in the intervention to aid the hosts of the party at Cana, but more especially in the words of

the Magnificat, echoing the song of Hannah in 1
Samuel 2. Perhaps no bolder social proclamation
occurs in the New Testament than that attributed
to Mary. She manifested both a familiarity with
and a concern for the downtrodden, the hungry,
and the lowly. They will be raised on high, she insisted, while their oppressors receive the consequences of their acts and omissions.

She was a woman with a finely integrated
sense of the totality of life, not limited to some sup-
posed bodiless spirituality. Rather, she *exulted* in
God while displaying a mighty concern for the
physical needs of the human family.

She was a woman of profound faith, support and stability. The Magnificat reflects a
bedrock belief in the promise of God. Under the
cross of Golgotha and in the upper room at
Jerusalem, she displayed a courage that sustained
others when she was bereaved.

She had a keen perception of the identity of
God. Whether or not the Magnificat be taken as
Mary's literal words, the fact that the Lucan account attributes them to her reflects some ap-
propriateness for contemporaries in having this
woman to report such thoughts.

The God she portrayed:

Shows mercy without end, calling humanity along ways it might not itself have
chosen.

Confuses the proud: those who fancy
themselves exempt from insecurity, from
self-scrutiny, and from the complexity of
life's flow.

Penetrates to the inmost heart of things and is not mocked by the majesty of thrones, nor the dizzy use of power or talent for its own sake.

Burns with care over the hungry and those who lack the resources that lead toward a fuller life—a life in which each person may revel both in the creator and the creation as well.

Stands in fidelity by his word, pointing to a future that is ever so sure in its direction, ever so unknown in its ways.

Not only is reflected, but magnified in the souls and flesh and bodies and emotions and movements and longings and joys of all people.

To follow the life and the way of the mother of the Lord is thus not to end up in a draining sentimentality; it is, rather, to discover a critical and mature spirituality. To follow this woman, whom Cardinal John Henry Newman liked to call simply "St. Mary," is to become aware of the demands of faith for the gradual stretching of the limits of the possible.

Mary did not lead an insulated life. She went through the dull, weary, sometimes distraught days that we too endure. Like us she had occasional glimpses of the gathered greatness that God allows us to see at times. But having the fullness of grace, she perfectly integrated her joys and struggles into a consistent tissue of meaning, goodness and service. She was not a person of soul

or spirit alone. Nor just body. Nor just emotion.
Nor just solitude. Nor just relationships. Rather,
she was what we must become: total.

hope

◆ to struggle in peace: an Easter mandate

Like a terrible contagion, fear spread about and seized the early Christian community time and again in the post-resurrection days. We see it and hear it everywhere in the New Testament accounts. Those who charge Christianity with projection and wish-fulfillment and security-seeking might do well to look here for a refutation of their theses. While there is doubtlessly joy in the resurrection narratives, we find the principal witnesses "half overjoyed, half terrified" in Matthew's account.

Some think they were frightened because their leader had recently been executed and they might be next. That is a fairly reasonable supposition, yet the fear seemed to increase as the news got better. It is precisely the resurrection that frightened them.

Others suggest then that they were frightened because they were uncertain and did not understand. Perhaps. But another possibility exists: maybe the disciples were frightened in part because they understood all too well. The good news of the resurrection of Jesus was not only about the ongoing life of their friend; it was not only a vindication in a political skirmish. It was an event with immense human, even cosmic implications.

And who was in the middle of it all? Who was being asked to internalize and share and spread this reality? The frightened followers—not the great intellectual or political leaders; not the finest writers of the age; not those most renowned for their asceticism and courage. All of those came later. In the beginning, the most earthen or fragile of containers were chosen: the stumbling, halting, fearful, unfaithful, lazy, impetuous men and women who had seen so much of it all happen.

"As the Father has sent me, so I send you" (Jn 20:21, NAB). This was an extraordinary mandate. The Father had sent Jesus to consecrate the world to a new vision of meaning, to a profoundly new way of looking at things. The disciples were now called to see and lead others in turn—to see a depth and possibility in living that many thought impossible. They were to insist that life is more than it merely seems to be, to insist that death itself is a process, a transition and not a finality.

Jesus had been sent into the world to "bring the good news to the poor, to proclaim liberty to captives and to the blind new sight, to set the downtrodden free, to proclaim the Lord's year of favor" (Lk 4:18-19). Now the disciples were sent to continue the task as the Christ had been sent.

It now became the lifework of those disciples to proclaim both cross and resurrection; to assert the power of direction in life over aimless drift; of meaning over absurdity; of life over death. The very account of scripture that relates the sending of the disciples to the mission of Jesus also indicates the costliness of the Easter joy, the painful price of resurrectional peace. As Jesus meets with his followers in the post-resurrection narrative he performs the singular gesture of showing them his scars. It is in this context that he speaks the words "peace be with you" (Jn 20:21). His peace is to be one of tireless struggle for the good in which the messengers may never weary of doing what is right. The peace of Easter, with its joy, was the dramatic conclusion to all that had gone before.

The days surrounding the passion of Jesus witness experiences and events that ran the gamut of many of the basic human emotions: the tenderness and treachery at the farewell meal of Holy Thursday; the agony and bravery of Good Friday; the expectancy and sorrow of Holy Saturday. It is only when we realize in the deepest way that those days of the Lord are also *our* days, that we can begin to sense the power of faith in our lives.

Only ~~when we struggle in~~ the peace of Easter ~~will we be able to~~ cast out fear ~~as a para~~lyzing ~~force in our lives.~~ "~~F~~ear is useless," said Jes~~us. "What is needed is trust"~~ (Mk 5:37). In that personal and primal trust alone does Easter faith ~~become our faith, and~~ Jesus' resurrection our own rising ~~at last~~ to life.

◆ quo vadis?

Our days come and go. The summers roll around; the winters, the summers again: seasons of a life. Where are they taking us? We do well to wonder.

Living ladens us with experiences: joys and sorrows, hopes and desperations. Within and around ourselves we observe strength and weakness, kindness and cruelty, growth and decay. The cycles, like the seasons, so often seem to repeat themselves: being born, growing, hurting, loving, hating, achieving, failing, tiring, dying. The Romans had a questioning phrase that catches something of it—*quo vadis*—where are you going? and to what purpose?

These are questions we all ask eventually. Does life have intensity and meaning, or is it an endless and pointless round of toils—Shakespeare's and Faulkner's tale full of sound and fury, signifying nothing?

And yet, toil and troubles do not exhaust the range of our experiences. We meet compassion, forgiveness, justice, beauty, wisdom, wit and partial order along our winding ways as well. And some instinct as deep as life itself insists that such realities count far more than selfishness, bitterness, evil, ugliness, stupidity, moroseness and chaos. When Jesus drew his famous picture of true beatitude, he may have given voice to a revolutionary, often unpopular view of the world, but he also captured something that is printed deep in the human psyche. We may yet not be able to deny some of our finest secrets and instincts: we are all, in some sort, beatitude people.

We are drawn together as communities of faith and worship precisely because, no matter how haltingly or resistantly, we are somehow drawn to the spirit, vision and pulse of that Christ. His followers have always maintained that he is our one great human champion; the one whose heart beats in fullest and finest rhythm with the very heart of God.

It is now nearly two decades since the Second Vatican Council elaborated such a view of the Christ in *The Church in the Modern World*:

> The Lord is the goal of human history, the focal point of the longings of history and of civilization, the center of the human race, the joy of every human heart, and the answer to all its yearnings.

> He was the image of the invisible God. For by his incarnation, Christ has united himself in some fashion with every human being.

> He worked with human hands.
> He thought with a human mind.
> He acted by human choice.
> He loved with a human heart.

Throughout history, there have been countless people who have walked the way of this Christ; they shared his shaping vision of reality. In that perspective alone, they have sensed, the word *worthy* could be written fully and finally across a human life. Christian faith discovered not only that Jesus was in his attitudes and approaches to life all that humanity could become (true man); it also found that he was the fullest disclosure of the mystery at the very heart of a loving deity (true God).

In following "The Way"—one of Christianity's most ancient titles—people have found frustration in a community that often seems to forget the sacred message that it bears. But more importantly, believers have found the truest ground of wholeness and hope in a world of all too frequent brokenness and desolation. In the cross, believers perceive the harsh reality of suffering in the world. But in the resurrection they learn that the cross points to victory over futility, rather than signifying despair.

In community, prayer, scripture, sacrament, especially the Eucharist, the believer reaches for—and in turn is touched by—the utter source of unwearied love, compassion, forgiveness and hope. If we join ourselves profoundly to such a community of church, we too can touch mystery and be touched by it. Life, even our own sometimes dreary excuse of a life, can take on shape, can acquire confidence and power; can face disorder, decay, and even death itself.

We can come to know where we are going, even if we are not sure how. *Quo vadis?*

The Christian answers: along the path of life and death trod by the Lord before me and for me.

If we follow him through the darkness, we may also follow him into the light. And beyond this life? There is a comfort, to be sure, in the proclamation of 1 Corinthians 2:9 echoing Isaiah and Jeremiah, that there awaits for us "the things that no eye has seen and no ear has heard, things beyond the mind of man, all that God has prepared for those who love him."

But one can also find insight in the judgment

of the American poet whom no one has ever accused of being conventionally religious, Walt Whitman. Underneath everything known, he insisted, was "nativity." And what exists beyond the known? "In the Song of the Rolling Earth" Whitman wrote:

> I swear I see what is better than to tell the best
> it is always to leave the best untold.

It is the mystery that lures us on. And that mystery, Christianity maintains, has a name and a heart and an invitation to offer: come, follow me.

patience

◆ endurance

George Bernard Shaw once proposed a tongue-in-cheek epitaph for himself: "I knew that if I stayed around long enough, something like this would happen." More than a little of this genteel fatalism has taken hold in the culture we recognize as our own. Life is, at its best, keeping creatively engaged until the undertaker arrives. That is patience in its most beneficent contemporary rendering.

Christianity offers a variant reading of the ancient virtue of patience: it points not to emptiness, but to plenitude; not to barrenness, but to a kind of cosmic pregnancy.

Thomas Merton sought this grace of patience in monastic life and he set out to share it with his impatient time. He knew as well as any of the classic Christian writers down the centuries that patience is neither passivity nor resignation. Christian patience has a potency to it, a sense of the provisional, as Rahner styles it; a kind of *hidden wholeness* in Merton's phrase. The meekness that faith so highly prizes, then, is not so much utter pliability as it is power for the good held in reserve.

Never have a people, never has an age so needed to channel its reserved power properly. Never has leadership, both in society and in the movement called Christianity, so desperately needed to be reflective or contemplative within the middle of frantic activity and busyness. Author James Carroll has called contemplation the doubting of that which seems obvious to everyone. It is the refusal to live on the surface of things.

In the very beginning of the Christian drama the principal human actors did not start by writing a statement of purpose. They did not set up committees, or draw up job descriptions. All these distasteful but necessary things came later. Rather, the earliest Christian leaders began by taking time out. They began, paradoxically, with a pause. They returned to the upper room. They considered the dangers and risks of their position. They prayed. They reflected. They waited.

All of us have our own particular upper room. But we each have also our own Jerusalem to which we must return, where we must serve, where we must let our patience be put in the crucible. We never achieve or attain once and for all. Call it the Freudian thanatos. Call it original sin. Call it what you will. Our lives are "comma" and not "period" affairs. We are always unfinished products. To some extent, we are our own insufficiencies. Finality signifies death, while process and flexibility bespeak life.

It was John Lennon who insisted that life is what happens to us while we busy ourselves with other plans. Life is a flow and not a frozenness. Rarely do we do anything in this world "once and for all." Certainly we do not cast out evil on such a basis; it needs resisting over and over again as time, in its mystery, goes by.

Like Rabbi Heschel and Dorothy Day, both of whom he admired so deeply, Merton thought that one of the great gifts the believer could bring to the age was a redemptive sense of time—time that would be committed and passionate, yet patient and enduring. Merton's close friend, David

Steindl-Rast, a monk and a psychiatrist, reported after Merton's death on a conversation they had held on this very subject. It was Merton who spoke:

> The reason why we don't take time is a feeling that we have to keep moving. This is a real sickness. Today time is commodity, and for each of us time is mortgaged. We experience time as unlimited indebtedness. We are sharecroppers of time. We are threatened by a chain reaction: overwork—overstimulation—overreaction—overcompensation—overkill. And yet . . . Christ has freed us.
>
> We must approach the whole idea of time in a new way . . . We live in the fullness of time. Every moment is God's own good time, his *kairos*. The whole thing boils down to giving ourselves a chance to realize in prayer that we have what we seek. We don't have to rush after it. It is there all the time, and if we give it time, it will make itself known to us.
>
> The best way to pray is: stop. Let prayer pray deep within you, whether you know it or not.
>
> (From *Thomas Merton, Monk,* edited by Brother Patrick Hart.)

If the Christian people are to pray, then, they too must learn *to stop.* That is why they take time out around a table that is at once common and extraordinary. At the Eucharist they discover the sacred space of Christian identity. There too they experience the sacred time of the endurance of God. They learn to have patience with the provisional, for patience is the twin of faith.

◆Christian karma

For all their immense and sometimes bewildering diversities, the major religions of the world have this much in common: they all accept the evident fact that humanity at large and each of us in particular has a fundamental flaw. For all that is good, right and true about us, it is also true that there is something out of tune, out of step, unfinished, incomplete, broken.

All the religions tell us that a fundamental flaw is marring humanity. They all also try to help us find remedies or salvation in the midst of that situation. In the Western religions, for instance, Christianity's Lent, Judaism's Yom Kippur and Islam's Ramadan, all come to grips directly with this shadow side of our natures and our choices.

The religions differ among themselves, and within themselves, on the question of where that flaw is primarily located. Some say it is in the way we think or perceive things; thus the intellect becomes the culprit. Others place the fault in our will or our emotions. Some Enlightenment and 19th-century secular religions placed the fault outside ourselves, in society or the environment or in genetic structure. All these approaches, of course, have a cogency and a degree of truth.

The Western religions in particular situate a major difficulty in the fact that we allow our desires all too often to exceed our needs and possibilities. Thus we write the scripts for our own frustration and unhappiness. Early Buddhism goes much farther than this in its estimate; it urges its adherents to cast desire itself out of their lives, as far as humanly possible.

In extending their cautions, Judaism, Christianity and Islam do not argue against high aspirations. Part of the moral drive of our nature is to push ourselves to become more than we presently are. Still, the religions urge the faithful to a chastened realism. We all need to live with certain limitations and to "own" them as our own personal context.

People have been known to waste lifetimes wishing that they were someone else, possessed of different faces, bodies, talents, minds, nationalities or personalities. In longing to be something that they are not, they undercut all those things that they uniquely have the power to be.

The beginning of good spirituality is to accept the self, not in the sense of apathy or mediocrity, but as precisely and intensely one's own. For in a very serious sense, healthy love of this primal self, both in its roots and the possibilities of its reach, is at the same time a love of the God who called it into this-being: now, and no other time; here and no other place.

Hinduism, the parent religion of Buddhism, teaches its adherents the doctrine of Karma: the moral necessity to be faithful to one's time and place in the recurring cycles of life, known as samsara. There may be a certain sorrow associated with one's karma, for it limits one's options and the range of possibilities. And yet, there is a power and consolation as well. In knowing and existentially affirming one's own special being, there is also identity, stability and freedom from formlessness.

It is entirely possible that our society at large is now doing us more harm than good by trying to foster unreal expectations in people. Our advertising, our films, our pop-psychologies all tell us at times in not so subtle ways that something like total happiness is within our grasp if we only would use the right deodorant, wear the right suit, pull our own strings, win through intimidation, practice bed-hopping. The list is endless.

Religions have a different story to tell. They have a more complex and challenging reading of our lives and humanity. Limitations, discipline, suffering, sacrifice—these are essential and formative parts of our lives. Without them, our better selves will never emerge out of the lesser. We may never discover our own true identity.

Who we truly are is better by far than any lotions, fabrics, sophisticated airs or possessions could ever make us. For, even standing with the smudge and smells and scars of our humanity all about us, we are beloved of that very Lord whom Christianity describes at various times as parent, lover, brother and friend.

We are accepted. We are loved. We are challenged by this God. In the face of such tenderness, we Westerners, closet Puritans and workaholics to our core, are permitted to be gentle with ourselves.

questioning

◆ an epistle to the agnostics

A Dublin-born actress some years ago was being interviewed by a reporter who was amazed at finding a believing and practicing Catholic in the jet set of the arts.

"Do you accept the virgin birth?" he asked. "Do you go to church every week? Do you believe in the divinity of Jesus?" On and on he pressed.

At last, in weary desperation, the actress blurted out: "Yes, I believe the whole damned thing. Let's move on to actors' equity."

But what of those who somehow cannot accept it all? John may have had such people in mind in his first epistle:

> No one has ever seen God;
> but as long as we love one another
> God will live in us (4:12).

It is a startling admission that might well bring the reader up short in its obviousness and simplicity. We simply do not see this God whom we spend our lives trying to love and serve. We rather sense this God alive within us and around us through the divine creativity and love printed in our own being.

There is a good bit of not-knowing with every bit of knowing we do. This is true in science, the arts, medicine and every significant field of life. It is certainly true of our religious faith. There will always be dark zones. We grasp only in part. But this darkness, too, has its significance. We grasp only in part in order that we might be grasped as well.

Christian faith begins in a partial seeing, and it ends in the consummation most traditionally described as the beatific vision, the seeing of God face-to-face. But until that fullness, that pleroma, Christianity bids its believers to trust in and to work toward the light. T. S. Eliot wrote in *Choruses from "The Rock"* (1934):

> O Greater Light, we praise Thee for the
> less . . .
> We thank Thee for the lights that we have
> kindled . . .
> We see the light but see not whence it
> comes . . .
> Therefore we thank Thee for our little light
> that is
>   dappled with shadow.
> And when we have built an altar to the
> Invisible
>   Light, we may set thereon the little lights
> for which
>   our bodily vision is made.
> And we thank Thee that darkness reminds us
>   of light.

As early as the 19th century in the midst of the headiness of a "knowledge revolution," Newman had hymned an appreciation of partial knowing in "Lead, Kindly Light" with its assurance that one step at a time was sufficient in the "encircling gloom." John Lancaster Spalding, Newman's younger American contemporary and a co-founder of Catholic University of America, marvelled that educated people persisted in demanding that religion should be all brightness and clarity or else forfeit all claim to consideration.

see Griffiths Clinging

59

Religion, Spalding reminded his generation, was not meant to resemble the noonday sun without shadows. Rather, it is a small, steady candle that allows us to grope our way in the darkness. But *we* do the groping so that our struggles give birth to free selves. We might bear marks and scars, but we have also acquired a unique identity and personality: a face with which to meet the face of God.

Few observers of the human condition would expect moral perfection out of any individual all at once. Seasoned humanity-watchers know to look for trials and errors, approximations, discipline, and occasional compromise before anything like perfection comes into view. Similarly, coming to accept the total conceptual structure of Christianity—the ideas, dogmas and doctrines of faith—may be a process as well.

For all the turmoil and weaknesses in its history Christianity remains a precious treasure-house of perspectives on reality. It has one emphasis for us, perhaps, when we are younger; another when we are old. But if we persist in our seeing "through a glass, darkly," if we hold to our little lights of grace and faith, we will never be separated in life or in death from the utter source of light. And if we err or misunderstand in lesser things, we shall never, as Newman insisted, "sin against the Light."

Christianity at last is about *seeing*:

that dust and decay are not
all of reality, not even the half;

that there is always more to be seen
and said—within, around, and ahead of us.

The ancient faith would have us see that, even in this world of incredible contradiction and pain, we could not begin to describe darkness if there were no reality such as the light. The master symbol of Christian faith, the cross, stands as a reminder that there is no peace without pain; no accomplishment without labor; no crown, in the old phrase, without a cross.

Christianity is the proclaimer of costly redemption. But that which is cheaply gotten is cheaply held. That which is rendered us without our own readying is not truly ours at all. And so, in our partial seeing, we stand before the God whom we have never seen and await the fuller day when we shall know even as we are known.

Fundamental Things Apply

◈ hard sayings

> This sort of talk is hard to endure! How can anyone take it seriously?
>
> John 6:60 (NAB)

The sentiments of this biblical crowd are those of almost all sensitive people throughout Christian history who have tried to make scripture a serious part of their life and meaning. Scripture is a two-edged sword in many senses. It is God's word to us, a pillar of meaning in the midst of chaos; but it is also a possible source of frustration and misunderstanding. It may even, as Jesus acknowledges, shake our faith.

As biographer Peter Brown noted, St. Augustine turned quite naturally to the Bible to find wisdom, but it was a great disappointment to him. What Augustine read was cluttered with what was considered to be earthy and immoral stories from the Old Testament; and in the New Testament Christ was presented through long and contradictory genealogies.

Centuries later, the Protestant writer John Bunyan recorded a similar though less dramatic problem in his own approach to scripture. He wrote, "I have sometimes seen more in a line of the Bible than I could well tell how to stand under, and yet, at another time the whole Bible hath been to me as dry as a stick."

We need to be honest and we need to be realistic. We also need to be nourished by the life-giving, quickening word of God. Great figures in the Catholic and Protestant traditions, great lovers of the scripture, have at times found biblical talk hard to endure, difficult to grasp, a vexation—not only a blessing.

Consider these lines pulled from the New Testament without their contexts. They are hard words that we hardly take in their literal force, yet words that need reckoning.

"If your right eye should cause you to sin, tear it out and throw it away" (Mt 5:29).

"I say this to you: offer the wicked man no resistance" (Mt 5:39).

"If a man calls his brother 'Fool,' he will answer for it before the Sanhedrin" (Mt 5:22).

"I say this to you: do not swear at all" (Mt 5:34).

"You must call no one on earth your father . . . nor must you allow yourselves to be called teachers" (Mt 23:8-10).

"You must obey the governing authorities . . . and so anyone who resists authority is rebelling against God's decision" (Rom 13:1-2).

"Slaves be obedient to the men who are called your masters" (Eph 6:5).

"When you pray, go to your private room and, when you have shut your door, pray to your Father who is in that secret place" (Mt 6:6).

"If any man comes to me without hating his father, mother, wife, children, brothers, sisters, yes and his own life too, he cannot be my disciple" (Lk 14:26).

"It is the spirit that gives life, the flesh has nothing to offer" (Jn 6:63).

"So wives should submit to their husbands in everything" (Eph 5:24).

Time and time again when we approach scripture we are reminded that we must be wide rather than narrow in our approach. The Roman Catholic Church shares this wider perspective, this catholic approach, with the main-line churches of Protestantism and Orthodoxy. We dare not wrench a single line from context and use it as a weapon to state a point of view. The main-line Christian always reads the Bible with one eye on the text and one eye on the context.

The uncritical taking of scriptures, word by word, without the full use of all the human powers with which God has endowed us; the adapting of simple solutions and remedies to highly complex problems—these are escapes into a simplicity that never really existed. *7iptow of Husas it the thing*

We can never simply cut the cloth of the scriptures to suit the fabric of our own culture. Yet, since they are—in their total meaning—the searing, living words of God, they will not allow themselves to be imprisoned in exhausted forms of thought.

More than ever we see the need for the reality of the church, a living tradition that invites people to live out the deeper realities of faith in their lives. Such a church performs one of its most vital tasks when it allows the scriptures to come alive, age after age, under the lead of the spirit of wisdom. Through the experience of the Christian people, and with the critical and faithful researches of scriptural scholars, the Bible can most truly become the book of life.

That Bible can bring our lives balance, meaning, fulfillment and salvation; but we must truthfully face the fact that the scriptures can be touched at times with that same ambiguity with which grace itself seems so often to be inter-mingled. Even if the scriptures give us a merry chase in order to grasp them to the full; even if at times they lead us along insecure paths, we come back at last to making our own the words of Peter, "Lord, whom shall we go to? You have the message of eternal life."

simplicity

◆ the triumph of the ordinary

It is a sobering thought that during the world's great age of progress, the 19th century, over four billion human beings lived and died on the planet earth. Probably no more than two or three dozen of their names—such as Lincoln, Darwin, Queen Victoria, Bismarck—would be recognizable to even very literate audiences today.

In some ways, the interior of the earth itself can be viewed as a vast cemetery bearing around the remains, in one form or another, of all humanity from prehistoric eons through our own generation. The vast majority of these peoples have now behind them not the slightest physical reminder that they ever existed in the first place.

Such reflections are not meant to be macabre or morose. In fact, in the light of the religious traditions of the world, they open us to deeper perspectives of self-understanding and appreciation.

Clearly we were not made for the sake of fame, notoriety and unending earthly remembrance. Yet, ironically, so many citizens of the earth dash around in a frenzied search for just such passing accomplishments. The great world faiths instill a reverence and respect for the world and the human task in it. But they universally maintain that if we try to wrench from the earth our total meaning then we have misperceived reality.

We are made for more. The denial of this simple fact may well be the most original and yet most common of all sins.

We are creatures of dust and spirit, wonderfully and frightfully joined together. Our origins are low, our destinies high. Pascal wrote, "True religion must teach man's greatness and misery, and so beget self-esteem and self-contempt."

How peculiar we all are. We busy ourselves, cluttering up life with objects and projects and plans, many worthy, no doubt. But we then try to turn these things into testimonies of our own importance or greatness. We boast of those commodities that we can collect: dollars, cars, degrees, positions, conquests. Yet, trite and worn as the saying may be, it remains true: we can't ultimately clutch at things or take them with us. There are no pockets in shrouds. Or, as the French put it, the last suit needs no pockets. We have to learn to let go. In Dante's phrase, only in God's will is our peace.

The religious traditions remind us untiringly of the triumph of simplicity. The *Tao Te Ching* insists that we can never own the product of our labors, only the process. That process is tied to our very identities, to the mystery of the human heart. That mystery alone survives into eternity, bearing within it the greatness and intensities of the earth. It is not how *much* we do in life that matters so much as how *well* we do it.

Christianity in particular would have us know that all those activities and plans over which we fret may truly be good; they may be splendid and lead us to a more sensitive and humane way of living; they may lead us closer to God's very self. But all our projects and plans are means, not ends. They may *lead* to the ultimate, but they are *not* the ultimate. What does the child Christ tell us if not this? Christ, the human face of our God, comes to us without pretension, without display, without masks. The power of God is revealed in poverty. He comes to us in the drabness, the darkness, the dullness of daily life.

Most of us are called to the sanctity of seeming insignificance. We are to witness to the triumph of the ordinary, not of the obvious. In this, as in all crucial realities, Christ is both model and teacher. The ordinary contains the seed of greatness within itself. What do the parables report, what does the Eucharist signify, if not this profound reality? We are summoned both to action and contemplation, to simplicity and excellence. Like the Shaker community of 19th-century Kentucky, we would do well to seek dignity in work, tranquility in the spirit and excellence in all things.

Perhaps it was W. H. Auden who best captured and capsulized the balanced Christian insight into simplicity as he addressed Mary and Joseph in his 1944 *Christmas Oratorio* "For the Time Being":

> Blessed Woman,
> Excellent Man,
> Redeem for the dull the
> Average way
> That common, ungifted natures may
> Believe that their
> Normal vision can walk
> To perfection.

◆the riches of poverty

For some 20 centuries, the gospel has cut across the lives of Christian believers, bringing both consolation and challenge. The word has become flesh "so that they may have life and have it to the full" (Jn 10:10). By the startling fact of the incarnation, God assures us that human life and matter itself bears the possibility of the sacred; by its very integrity and autonomy, the material world can become a penetrating road to God.

And yet, while holding us to the preciousness and intensity of life, while urging us to cherish everything that is true, noble, good, honorable, worthy of praise, the gospel of Jesus cautions us that we have not here a lasting city. Humanity as we now know it fades like the grass or flower of the field. The same life that brings us its times of exaltation can also bring us low, "past pitch of grief" (Gerard Manley Hopkins). Life's dark side could make even the hardy St. Paul cry out: "What a wretched man I am! Who will rescue me from this body doomed to death?" (Rom 7:24).

The Christian community has ever borne in its corporate experience, in the life of prayer, sacrament and service, the answer to the agonizing question the Apostle posed: It is Christ alone, risen and still with us through his Spirit, who can reconcile life's ambiguities. To be in Christ is to be always in a process of growth—to be involved in painful farewells and surprising discoveries. If we are to bid good-bye to our own narrowness, our own clutching at absolutes other than the Lord himself, we will come more readily to the excitement of life

71

with God in the flesh; we will be more perfectly ready to experience the coming of the kingdom in mystery, day by day.

So it is that throughout Christian tradition, believers have sought ways of letting go, of releasing their grasp on all that could lead away from the fullness of life for each person. Whether in monasticism or fasting, in celibacy or lenten sacrifice, in almsgiving or acts of selfless charity, Christians have ever tried to affirm the very goodness of what they surrender by their willingness to cooperate with the Spirit in the work of transformation, of making all things new.

A life of poverty has always been an ideal in the Catholic faith—not because material beauty or moderate comfort or excellence is in any way evil. Quite the contrary. Precisely because there is so much in the material and corporeal make-up that is profoundly good, the Christian strives to make it greater than it already is, but putting it into perspective, by sharing it, and by personalizing it.

Because sharing and personal relationship are at the heart of the triune God, faithful people will strive to make all their personal material goods subservient to the growth of the person on all levels: physical, emotional, intellectual, social, spiritual. For this reason, believers hold only these realities that are personal and build up the dignity of the person with any degree of ultimacy. They will want to give of their own goods so that all might share in God's goodness. They will remember the frightening judgment of Jesus on the danger of riches, and on those who did not give of themselves to feed the hungry and clothe the naked.

They will remember the familiar words of St. John's epistle:

Anyone who says "I love God,"
and hates his brother,
is a liar,
since a man who does not love the brother
    that he can see
cannot love God, whom he has never seen.

1 Jn 4:20

And they will grapple with the powerful words quoted by the Second Vatican Council: "Feed the man dying of hunger, because if you have not fed him, you have killed him" (*The Church in the Modern World*).

All sensitive Christians with this clear witness of Lord and church ringing in their ears and hearts will want to come to grips with an abundant lifestyle, especially in America, in the midst of a world of hungry, lonely and oppressed peoples. At every level of life, they will want to follow in some balanced way the example of Christ in giving of themselves in time, talent, compassion and resources. Believers will not want to conform too closely to a society that merely seeks to enjoy and accumulate; rather, they will find creative ways to humanize that society, beginning with themselves.

And so Christians will want to attempt a workable lifestyle: one that allows them as much physical and psychological support as they need to be healthy, developing and well-rounded persons. Movies, art and concerts, books, travel—all within moderation, of course—open us to possibilities for deepening and sharing our personal worth. Recreation and sports also have their legitimate place in keeping us healthy and happy persons.

The old adage remains true: we can't give away what we haven't got. To project a style of life that impoverishes our own personality at any level makes us less able to share with others; to go to an extreme may be to deny for ourselves the very fullness we profess to wish for all persons. In short, a life of poverty must not become an impoverished life.

And yet, those who have chosen the path of the Christ will often want to have before them the urgency of starving people at home and abroad who can benefit directly from their concerns. And more than ever they will need to be informed, conscientious and vocal citizens in their own community and nation on a considerable range of social issues. Survival in a nuclear era, Third World development, the right of the unborn, the elderly, the unemployed and the marginal people, human and civil rights at home and abroad—these become critical moral issues for a people freed of cluttered lives so as to live for God's future.

In short, all believers without exception in this era are summoned not only to a moderate and balanced use of the goods of the earth; they are also called to be prophets who question things as they are and work for them as they might be. Abraham Heschel wrote in *The Prophets*:

> This is what the prophets discovered: history is a nightmare. There are more scandals, more acts of corruption, than are dreamed of in philosophy. But it would be blasphemous to believe that what we witness is the end of God's

creation. It is an act of evil to accept the state of evil as either inevitable or final. The way man acts is a disgrace. And it must not go on forever.

sin

◆ missing the mark

For many of the later years of his life, Daniel C.
Walsh, one of Thomas Merton's professors at
Columbia University, helped interview prospective
candidates for the Abbey of Gethsemani in Kentucky. Often he would ask the aspirants quite
bluntly why they wanted to be monks. If someone
were unfortunate enough to answer that he sought
to escape the evils of the earth, Walsh was ready
for the kill: "The evil in the world begins in
yourself," Walsh would tell them, "and you will
carry it with you wherever you may go." This is
not Puritanism or Jansenism. This is reality.

> Each of us is a sinner.
> We are not just victims of bad environment.
> We are not just insufficiently evolved.
> We sin.
> We miss the mark, to use the fine Greek
>   phrase *hamartia*.
> We turn our enormously good powers of love
>   in wrong
>   directions, to use Augustine's conception.
> We choose the lesser when the greater is
>   possible.
> We catch a glimpse of the light and then seek
>   out darkness.
> We get into ugly cycles of utter selfishness,
>   sloth, envy,
>   anger, gluttony, intemperance, pride,
>   blindness to
>   community needs, literal care-less-ness.
> We sin.

And that sinning has consequences. The

devastation that sustained evil can inflict on relationships, families and societies may be too obvious to need the telling. What may not be quite as obvious is the havoc that wickedness works on its performer. Sin diminishes the humanity of the sinner:

> It sets up a web of suspicion, vulgarity and distrust.

> It invites smallness, bitterness and jealousy, those acids that corrode the very vessels in which they are borne.

To mention sin without forgiveness is, for the Christian, roughly equivalent to discussing disease without noting the reality or possibility of health. Hard as it may be for many to believe, Christianity's greatest moral emphasis is on virtue, not vice. Both Aquinas and Dante, those giants of the medieval world, would wither at any contrary suggestion. God invests humanity with capacities and possibilities, they insisted; to undercut these powers and the good is sin in its ugliest sense. It is shutting off our most potent linkage to sharing in the life of God.

To cast out sin, though, is more than a matter of self-purgation. The cure of any serious illness must begin with an awareness of its desperateness and pain so that the sufferer enlists a physician's aid. The latter's task is then to draw forth from the body its own latent power of restoration and renewed vitality.

So it is with forgiveness, human or divine. It is not a mere forgetting of a few unfortunate acts of the past. No, what people have done or failed to do is stored in their own spiritual, psychic and social structures. The ill effects cannot be waved aside.

But the Christian concept of forgiveness assures us that we will never be overwhelmed or paralyzed by our past. We start from our pasts; we don't take up residence there. The reach of God's life into the human is an offer of the never revoked promise of an authentic future; it is creative possibility in the face of absurdity.

Perhaps the greatest of all sins is the failure to admit such a reality into our lives. The hardest doubt of all to conquer is surely not about the nonexistence of an abstract God; it is the doubt about the presence of God in one's own miserable old self. We find it hard to yield up the lurking fear that we can be welcomed into God's presence with the smells and scars of life's battles still very much upon us.

Forgiveness, then, is not a passive forgetting on the part of an indulgent God. Rather, it is an insistent demand not to wallow in the murkiness of our past. It is the refusal to be frozen out of that future to which God calls each of us by name and without exception.

Accepting this forgiveness from God means that we become channels of forgiveness for others; such is Christianity's next quirky demand. To be forgiven ourselves means unavoidably to see no one else as beyond forgiveness, beyond redemption.

In the ninth chapter of Matthew, Jesus is seen forgiving the sins of a paralytic and curing him of his physical ailment. He gives the cured man some pointed directions which are immediately followed, "The man got up and went home" (Mt 9:7).

There are allegorical implications here, if they be allowed. Forgiveness means getting up and going home. To be forgiven is no longer to crawl or grovel, but to rise to a position of human dignity and possibility.

Similarly, to be restored is to be no longer a stranger or alien, but a being with that most precious of possessions, a real home. We can then travel about as a helpful, friendly, challenging spirit precisely because we have an identity: a sense of dignity, direction, and destiny.

Being forgiven means that at last we can stand up; we can go all places with confidence because we have a home, a place where we can love and be loved, masks and pretenses down. To have religious faith is to leave the ranks of the homeless. To believe is to be a pilgrim—not a wanderer—on the troubled face of the earth.

 suffering

◆darker yet

1940 has quite rightly been called the darkest year in the history of Britain. The world seemed to be coming undone. The people of England stood alone, its allies knocked out of the war by Nazi power. By autumn the British were being blitzed nightly at a frightful cost of human life. With typical British realism and grit, the *Times* of London reported the devastating defeat in Crete late in May of that year with a portion of G. K. Chesterton's *Ballad of the White Horse*:

> I tell you naught for your comfort,
> Yea, naught for your desire,
> Save that the sky grows darker yet
> And the sea rises higher.
>
> Night shall be thrice over you,
> And Heaven an iron cope.
> Do you have joy without a cause,
> Yea faith without a hope?

The mood reflected in those somber days of war is never without an echo in the human heart. Even in times of peace, we experience the inevitability of suffering and evil. We come to realize that it is not only a case of explaining the suffering of the innocent, rather, we discover that more often than not, the innocent and the good suffer because they *are* innocent and good. The great central symbol of Christianity—the cross—gives poignant testimony to this fact. Struggle is at the heart of reality between the good and the bad and that drama is acted out in each of us. Yet, once the battle has been waged, once the victory has been won under the urging of grace, we truly *own* our virtue. We are innocent because we choose to be.

The Christian faith we claim, and which claims us, does not promise ease of accomplishment. That faith may see "the sky grow darker yet." It may see "heaven an iron cope," but it believes steadfastly that just as there is the pull to violence in each of us, there is also the childlike possibility for good. That faith calls us to welcome the child that lingers in each of us, the child unconquered by cynicism and despair.

These are not romantic musings; they are as real as competent philosophy, theology and psychology can acknowledge. Call them what you will, we each bear around in us a life force and a death force, eros and thanatos, a destructive and a creative side. It is our great task in life to master the shadow side, not deny it—to make it serve the better. We *need* our angers, our destructive energies, to wipe out all that should not be in our personal lives and our societies.

We are those beings that Milton called "darkly wise and rudely great." We harbor mysteries within ourselves, and choices as well. Which shall we finally be: the cynic or the child? The destructive or the creative? In these choices, in truth, there may be naught for our immediate comfort; they perplex, they puzzle and they sting. And yet to stare into the face of such decision is to discover the very Christ already gone before us: the one who chooses well and bids us to follow.

⬡lacrymae rerum

Sunt lacrymae rerum.

So said Virgil in one of the most profound and nearly untranslatable utterances of the *Aeneid.*

There are tears in things.

Life has a cutting edge.

Sorrow is threaded deep in the weave of all things human.

Suffering pervades all things. (The First Noble Truth of Buddhism.)

Sunt lacrymae rerum.

Earlier ages have found such statements to be merely evidential at face value. Americans by way of contrast, even down to this day, have had difficulty giving full adherence to such a creed. Not entirely surprising for a nation that asserts on its dollar bills that it ushered in "the new order of the ages."

This American instinct for innocence may often have elements of naivete or even willful blindness about it. Still, for all its secular pretensions, the nation that holds that, even with scars and flaws, it can hope for liberty and justice for all, is a nation undergirded not only by Enlightenment but by Jewish and Christian perceptions of life as well.

The biblical affirmations of both Judaism and Christianity (and of Islam too) are that the Creator God always calls humanity to life, always offering re-creating possibilities, even in the midst of seeming futility. The very one whom Christians call Lord, for instance, was one who insisted:

—that coherence outruns chaos;

—that life ultimately outwits death;

—that we can, with honesty and honor, in Rahner's fine phrase, say "Father" to incomprehensibility.

The great religions of the West join in their conviction that a personal God bears the reality of love as a primal, definitional fact. Christianity's St. John makes it all quite explicit in his devastatingly simple assertion that God is love. Such a love, incarnated in persons and histories, causes the world to be sacramental in nature:

—making life more intense

—making living more of a treasure

—helping to make God a presence in our lives rather than an abstraction.

Such a love, faith must admit, may wear many distressing disguises, even to the point that the cross, an emblem of shame, can become one of love's primal symbols. Yet, such a love can be tender without being sentimental. It can make demands without overwhelming the beloved. It can, as the poet Rainer Maria Rilke realized, live as well with questions as it can with answers. And when the final trump is played, the great religions insist, love is even stronger than death itself.

Things are more than they appear. The Beatitude discourse of Jesus makes a valiant test case of such a claim. The beatitudes show a world turned upside down. A Logos world. A world in which the central values are hope, justice, holiness, endurance and compassion. A world in which God guides each by name without exception to struggle and to peace.

Fundamental Things Apply

Things are not what they merely seem to be:
—We are most our own when we let go.
—We most possess when we refuse to clutch
and grasp.
—We are most alive when we refuse to fear
even death itself.

God gives to each of our lives a frame.
Within it we each paint an unrepeatable canvas of
life in its perplexity, humor and splendor. In paint-
ing the canvas, in living the life, we discover that
believing in fullness of life, even beyond the limitations of this one, seems neither far-fetched nor
desperate. Life and faith join to school us in this
fundamental fact: Life belongs ultimately to life.
And if there are tears in things, there are rejoicings
for things as well. It has often been said and is
worth saying again: the great mystery is not so
much that we suffer and die, but that we live in the
first place and have a rage to live long and well. We
are a people who revere energy, a people who
believe in ways often inarticulate and unaccount-
able, that the dance rather than decay is our
destiny.

Thomas Merton who knew much about suffering in his life and in his century wrote sagely at
the conclusion of *New Seeds of Contemplation*:

> No despair of ours can alter the reality of things,
> nor stain the joy of the cosmic dance which is
> always there. Yet, we are in the midst of it, and
> it is in the midst of us, for it beats in our very
> blood, whether we want it to or not.

> We are invited to forget ourselves on purpose
> . . . to cast our awful solemnity to the winds,
> and to join in the general dance.

trustfulness

◆cynics and children: a Christmas meditation

Possessed of an extremely ugly temperament, British novelist Evelyn Waugh was once asked how it was possible for him to be a Christian, a Catholic, and yet so appallingly unkind to people. "Only imagine," he replied, "how nasty I might be if I were not a Christian."

Oddly enough, this may be an apt starting point for a meditation on the feast of Christmas. How easy it is to be a cynic in this season. All the high hopes—the innocence and possibility of new life, peace on earth, the light penetrating the darkness, the presence of God to the world—these often seem bitterly obsolete by early January.

But what if there were no Christmas? What if we failed to affirm those great truths and hopes for which it stands? How nasty might we, in fact, become? If we failed to light these candles yet again, what a darkness of curses and distress would be our lot. Still, the cynic says, Christmas is for children. Adults are too seasoned, too jaded, to hold the feast to its promises.

Still, there are those who would maintain that Christmas is most especially the feast of cynics *and* the feast of children. The nativity admits all the evil and brokenness that the cynic laments, while it affirms that all our brokenness, all our vulnerability is but a beginning, a starting place, a birth. Christmas affirms partialness and the incompleteness in our lives for what they truly are: not just trials, but benedictions.

Both the cynic and the child have felt fear.

But the child has the primal sense of trust and security as well, usually in the person of the parent. Christmas coexists with fear, but says that the world is worth at least a minimum of trusting.

Both the cynic and the child know about loneliness. But the child knows that tenderness and love are worth wailing and seeking after. Christmas says that the earth and its people, with all their strange intensities, are still worth befriending.

Both the cynic and the child have experienced pain and unhappiness. But the child, as if by some mysterious instinct, knows that there is more to it than that. Dr. Kübler-Ross tells of Majeanek concentration camp children drawing butterflies on the walls before their execution in 1945. Only later did she herself learn that these were cross-cultural symbols of rebirth. Christmas reminds us that the world is still worth crying about. It has such a long way to go. But it has so much good hidden inside awaiting our discovery.

Both the cynic and the child have been busy at countless little jobs. The cynic ponders whether any of it is worthwhile. The child is not possessed of such strange considerations, but is merged with the moment. Christmas says that we may work in peace because our task is not ours alone. We don't have to work always harder and longer only to find our security and satisfactions fewer. Christmas and the child say that the world is worth playing about. None of us has to take ourselves too seriously. None of us has to stay locked in our awful seriousness.

Finally, both the cynic and the child know

about complexity. The cynic proclaims it daily and
maintains it all to be chaos. But the children never
stop asking questions because they sense that there
is a freshness in the world, "deep down things."
They always want to know more about things and
how they work. Christmas says that the world is
worth wondering about. We can always be cor-
rected like a child; can admit error without
devastation and start again.

Christmas has a special message for the
child and the cynic in all of us: "Unless you change
and become like little children you will never enter
the kingdom of heaven" (Mt 18:3). We are all, and
always, beginners.

The world is worth trusting and befriending
and crying about and laughing and playing in, and
wondering about. Why? Just because it is not ours
alone. It has come to us like a gift, both from the
people who have lived before us and the God who
is creating still. The hopes and fears of all the years
have truly met, and cynics and children may romp
together at Christmas, in a rare frenzy of freedom.

virtue

◆ life in the fast lane: a prime consideration

"Life in the Fast Lane" not only names a rock song from a few years ago, it also designates a way of life in the United States, a nation of the most mobile people in recorded history. Never have a people changed residence, profession, spouse or friendships on such an accelerated basis. Americans venerate not only change, but speed and size as well.

For all the economic advantages and social opportunities such lifestyles may bring about, people must also pay a frightful price. A country of disintegrating family structures and of people looking with increasing urgency for roots and purposes, we have become the international capital for nervous breakdowns as well as early heart attacks and strokes.

Is there any action the individual can take—especially the Christian believer—to redeem the frantic times? First and foremost, people of faith must keep alive a sense of affirmation that adversity can be turned to opportunity. They need to be evident among those who become knowledgeable about issues in all their complexity, and who are willing to help confront them in a competent and conscientious way. In short, believers need to be personally, morally and socially vigilant.

One of the most effective counter positions to the false urgencies and misplaced intensities of our time is for Christian people to begin to cast out from their own lives the forces of diminishment.

Put another way, they must be about the business of achieving their *own* prime of life so that they can be more effective in service to society.

In the history of its spirituality, Christianity has developed various methods of self-scrutiny and examination of conscience. As early as the first-century *Didache,* Christians were reminded that the way of life and the way of death stand before each individual. The Christian was bidden, in very practical terms, to choose life. Medieval writers from at least the time of Augustine spoke of the purgative, illuminative and unitive approaches to spiritual life. Ignatius Loyola was even more systematic in his late 16th-century *Spiritual Exercises.*

What follows here is an examination for occasional use in fast lane times. This examen is by no means suggested to be remotely on a par with any of the spiritual methods just noted. Rather, it is meant as a starting point for self-awareness and change in a time of rapid social, technological and even theological change:

Personability

In a computerized, privatized and mechanized age, can the believer bring respect for uniqueness and personality to the fore? Can the individual afford time to *listen* to the needs, ideas and feelings of others? The "ministry of the listening heart," as author Jerome Neufelder styles it, may be the most difficult discipline of our busy time. Can the faithful person be so free of the self-obsessions of each day as to be truly present to the moment, its people, its situations and its surprises?

Renewal

Do believers show the same kindnesses to themselves that they try to make possible for others? Can they take time to rest, to exercise, and to play? Or are they trapped in busy celebrations of their own indispensability? Do they treasure learning and diversity, and the need to renew mind, body and spirit?

Involvement

Before the individual can think or act effectively on a community, national or world issue, there comes first the serious obligation of acquiring thorough information. This suggests both a wide, comprehensive awareness of many issues and a specialized knowledge and stance of action in regard to perhaps one or two areas. Does the faithful Christian have the stamina for the long haul—to continue to be concerned about the basic issues of the time—from the neighborhood to the nation? Can such commitments endure, in and out of season; can they survive fads as well as opposition?

Meditation

In the middle of all the energies and agendas of a life, is there time for serious prayer, meditation, reading of the scriptures and the better spiritual writers? When everyone else is simply busy, can believers know the reason for all the busyness in the first place? Can they translate their grounds for hope and elemental trust into the lives of others? In ways that are neither oppressive or self-righteous, can they lead others to sense that there is a personal reality at the heart of the universe, and that there is a force loose for good in the world that is not itself the world?

Expertise

How competent are believers in their own professional, vocational and parental roles? Are lifelong learning, precision and expertise among the primary values of the individual? Can the professions themselves—such as medicine, law, politics, social work, teaching, or economics—benefit significantly from the presence of the competent, conscientious professional?

◈ the shattering of narrow imaginings

There is a mystery loose in the world.
There always has been.
It is the Christian perspective that
    such mystery has now revealed itself
    most powerfully and persistently:
    it has a face.

The word of this mystery
became our very flesh:
    lived among us,
    served,
    loved,
    suffered,
    endured,
    broke through to life's heart.

With the account of the Last Supper of Jesus,
    we begin to realize:
    the terrible price he had to pay;
    the awful resistance he met in his doing of
      good;
    the crushing betrayal and abandonment
      by those who were considered his
      dearest friends.

But in the midst of all this turmoil,
He *stood* when there was every reason to fall.
He embodied:
    patience,
    compassion,
    faith,
    humility,
    justice.

Do this in memory of me, he said.
But not in memory of him alone.

All the broken bodies of history,
All the spilled blood,
All the Veronical veils of the teeming
    humanity of all time—
All these are brought to mind and heart as
    well, whenever
        Eucharist takes place among us.

At such a moment, the time and the timeless
    meet.
The shaping memories and stories of a faithful
    people
        are recited by the lips and rekindled in the
            heart.

Whenever they hear again the passion
    accounts of the Lord,
Christians understand anew that there is much
    more to life's story—
And to each and every personal story—
Than its many contradictions and
    diminishments.

To these realities, our lives must bear witness
    from inside out.
Whenever we eat of that body,
Whenever we drink of that blood,
We take significance into ourselves.
We join our stories to that of Jesus the Christ.

We become his true friends.
By that very act, we become friends:
        to the earth,
        to its people,
        to its history,
        to its future.

    In his life, death and resurrection, Jesus
refigured for all time the human equation. This

work of undermining the forces of diminishment and death had been foreshadowed in his early ministry in the Beatitude discourse. There he turned conventionality upside down in his imaging of those factors that make humanity happy and great.

Now, as his life drew to a close, Jesus' vision of reality was put to its direct test. The ugly force of all the primal sins bore down on him. Yet he resisted with all his might. Consider:

The *pride* of Peter enshrined in his overconfident phrase: "Lord I will never disown you."

Jesus, by contrast, showed a *humility* and a self-abandonment at Gethsemane—"Let it be as you, not I, would have it."

The *sloth* of the sleeping apostles, Peter, James and John; while the *energies* of Jesus were focused, directed and exercised even to the seeming desolation of the end.

The *intemperance* of a festival crowd that gave Jesus a frenzied welcome to Jerusalem only to call for his crucifixion soon thereafter. The Christ in that same week took *a simple meal* with his friends and transformed the meaning of food and friendship.

The *lust* and misuse of the flesh, as well as the sadistic delight of the soldiers over the broken body of their victim; while Jesus, by contrast, showed *compassion* even for the ear severed from the soldier by the impetuous Peter. Even at the end of all the agony, he is still concerned with the forgiveness of his tormentors.

The *greed* of a Judas for his silver and of soldiers for a cloak; while Jesus promised to *share* a kingdom with a common thief.

The *envy* of the pharisees and sanhedrin; while Jesus supported and *encouraged* the sorrowing people he met on his path to the hill.

The *anger* of the crowd and the trial lawyers. Compare to this the quiet *resolution* of Jesus on the witness stand.

Small wonder that this time can be in full truth called a passover. In his life—and most specially in his death—Christ shattered the narrowness of our human imaginings about the range of human possibility.

In his living and dying, Jesus gave us a model and example. In his rising and sending of the Spirit, he has gifted us further with the power of ultimate passage from darkness to light, and from bondage to freedom. The mystery loose in the world is at last unleashed in ourselves. Our narrowness dies the death. And we are reborn into immensity.

afterword

a prayer for fundamental things

Since then my God, thou hast
So brave a Palace built; O dwell in it,
That it may dwell with thee at last!
Till then, afford us so much wit;
That, as the world serves us, we may serve
    thee,
And both thy servants be.

George Herbert
(1593-1633)